WHY IS THERE RACISM?

Written by Anita Ganeri
Illustrated by Renia Metallinou

London Borough of Enfield	
91200000827410	
Askews & Holts	22-Jan-2025
J305.8 JUNIOR NON-FI	
ENSOUT	

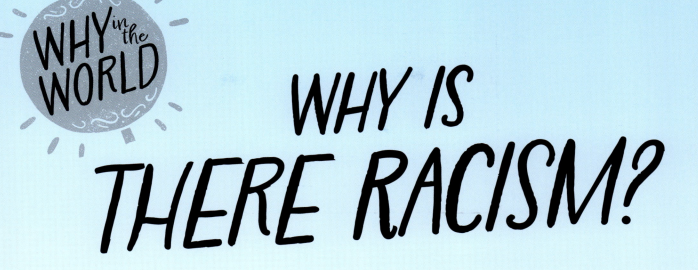

WHY IS THERE RACISM?

Have you ever been picked on or called a name? Have you ever been called a name because of the colour of your skin or perhaps how you speak?

Treating someone badly or unfairly because of their skin colour, or where they are from, is called racism.

This book looks at what racism is, how it affects people, and what is being done to stop it.

Race is a way of grouping people. It can be based on skin colour and the different ways people look.

If someone is called names because of race, it is called racism.

But racism isn't just about unkind or hurtful words.

Racism is also about the way people behave. They behave badly or unfairly because people are different from them.

Here's what racism might look like:

Leaving someone out of a game

Not sitting next to them in the dining hall

Taking or damaging their things

Hurting them physically – pushing, shoving or hitting.

Why are some people racist?

They think it's a way of being part of the crowd.

They hear or see others being racist and copy them.

They're afraid of people who are different to them.

For example, they don't understand that some people wear special clothes as signs of their religion.

Racism is about judging people, even if they don't actually know them or haven't ever met them.

For hundreds of years, people have been treated differently because of skin colour. In some countries, many people with lighter skin thought they were better than people with darker skin.

Some people still believe that racist ideas like this are true today even though most people know that they are not.

Treating someone differently because of their skin colour is wrong.

In the past, in some countries, people of colour were treated as second-class citizens.

They were kept apart from white people by strict laws.

People of colour had separate schools and restaurants. They had to sit in different parts of buses and trains. If they sat in the 'wrong' place, they could be fined or put in prison.

Many brave people worked hard to get these unfair laws changed.

Throughout history, people have left their homes and moved to other countries.

People move to find work, for safety, to explore or just to experience different places.

We all share the same planet. We understand more about other people and cultures than ever before.

We enjoy sharing each other's stories, traditions and food.

We need to respect and learn about different people.

Some people say racist things without thinking. They say that they don't mean any harm. They don't think what they're saying is wrong.

It doesn't matter who is being racist, adults or children. All racism is bullying. It can make a person feel upset, scared, angry or ashamed.

It can make a person feel that they're not good enough.

In many countries around the world today, racism is against the law.

It is the law to treat everyone equally, whatever their race or skin colour.

But sometimes, these laws get broken by people who are racist. They do not want people who are different from them to live in the same country.

They may use violence or damage someone's home or business.

For years, many people around the world have worked hard to stop racism. Some of them even put their lives in danger, or ended up in prison.

Today, there is still racism. Anti-racist groups still hold marches and events to spread their message about equality for everyone.

Racism can only be stopped if everyone works together.

Racism is very hurtful, and speaking out about it can be hard. If someone is racist, don't keep it to yourself.

Tell your parents, teachers or another adult you trust.

Look out for others. If someone looks upset, ask them if they are okay.

There are no excuses for racism.
Racism is never okay.

Everyone has the right to be treated with respect.

Everyone should be valued for who they are.

Everyone is different, and that's a good thing. Imagine how boring life would be if everyone was the same.

Let's all work together to make sure that everyone is included, and treated the same.

Notes for parents, teachers and carers

Racism can happen at any time, and anywhere. It can be subtle and unthinking, or deliberate and pointed but it always has a devastating effect on victims. For children, it can be especially difficult to deal with. They might find it hard to understand why someone would want to be racist towards them. They might feel upset, angry, anxious, sad and afraid. It can have a hugely detrimental effect on their sense of identity, and self esteem.

Standing up to racism, or speaking out about it, takes a great deal of courage. Racism is a form of bullying in which the bully tries to intimidate the victim. Children may be too afraid to speak, at home or at school, and will need reassurance. It is vital that they can identify someone they can trust – a parent, teacher or an organisation – and know that they will be listened to. In class, a carefully managed discussion about why racism happens, how it makes people feel, and what to do if they see someone being racist, or experience racism themselves, can help to reinforce the school's existing anti-bullying policies.

Racism is often based in ignorance. Talking to children, and answering any questions they may have, about difference and diversity can help to avoid misunderstandings. In our increasingly multicultural society, it is essential that children (and adults, of course) learn to value difference, and to treat other people with kindness, tolerance and respect. Accepting that human beings are not all the same, and celebrating each one as unique, is a huge step towards tackling racist attitudes before they become entrenched.

Glossary

anti-racist – against racism

bullying – when a person says or does things to hurt or frighten someone else

fined – ordered to pay a sum of money as punishment for breaking the law

race – a way of grouping people, often based on skin colour or appearance

Further reading

Lift-the-flap Questions and Answers about Racism
by Jordan Akpojaro and Vici Layhane (Usborne Publishing, 2022)

My Skin, Your Skin: Let's talk about race, racism and empowerment
by Laura Henry-Allain MBE and Onyinye Iwu (Ladybird, 2021)

Racism and Intolerance (Children in our World)
by Louise Spilsbury and Hanane Kai (Wayland, 2018)

Websites

BBC NEWSROUND
A guide for children about what racism is, where it comes from and what you can do to stop it. With first-hand accounts, and advice on what to do if you're upset by what you see or hear.
www.bbc.co.uk/newsround/52965984

UNICEF (United Nations Children's Fund)
A UNICEF guide for parents about how to talk to their children about racism, at different ages, and how to reinforce and celebrate diversity.
www.unicef.org/parenting/talking-to-your-kids-about-racism

Index

anti-racism 23

behaviour 8, 9

bullying 19

cultures 17

feelings 19

laws 14, 15, 20, 21

race 6, 7, 20

religion 11

respect 17, 26

skin colour 6, 13

traditions 17

First published in Great Britain in 2024
by Hodder & Stoughton
Copyright © Hodder & Stoughton
Limited, 2024

All rights reserved.

HB ISBN: 978 1 4451 8766 2
PB ISBN: 978 1 4451 8767 9

Printed in China

Franklin Watts
An imprint of Hachette Children's Group
Part of Hodder & Stoughton
Carmelite House
50 Victoria Embankment
London EC4Y 0DZ

An Hachette UK Company
www.hachette.co.uk
www.hachettechildrens.co.uk

With thanks to Emma Zipfel for her comments on this book